JUNIOR GREAT BOOKS

PEGASUS SERIES
VOLUME 1

The Great Books Foundation

A nonprofit educational corporation

First Printing

9   8   7   6   5   4   3

Printed in the United States of America

Published and distributed by

The Great Books Foundation

A nonprofit educational corporation

35 East Wacker Drive, Suite 2300

Chicago, Illinois 60601-2298

Note to the At-Home Reader

Read the assigned story aloud, making sure your child can see the text and pictures as you read. Ask your child to say the underlined phrases in the book with you. Whenever the character "G.B." (pictured above) appears, you will know that you should ask your child the question in the box. Give your child time to think through and talk over his or her answer. Whenever you can, ask your child **why** he or she gave that answer. Keep in mind that these are open-ended questions for which there are no single right answers. When G.B.'s question calls for an answer to be marked, help your child do so.

When you have finished the reading, ask your child what question he or she has about the story. Write this question on the lines provided at the end of the selection.

For the "Fanciful Animals" poetry unit, read "The Quangle Wangle's Hat" once through, asking your child to chorus the underlined phrases with you. Then read the poem a second time, discussing G.B.'s questions as they occur.

Your child will read and discuss the other two poems, "The Owl and the Pussy-Cat" and "Teddy Bear," later, in class, but feel free to enjoy these poems together at any time.

The blank pages in this book are for activities that will be completed in class. Encourage your child to show you his or her work when each unit is finished.

CHESTNUT PUDDING

IROQUOIS FOLKTALE

In a small lodge deep in the woods an old woman lived with her grandson. Every day she would cook food for the little boy, but she herself would never eat.

One evening, when the fire was hot and potatoes and moss were simmering, the boy asked his grandmother to sit down and have supper with him. "I will eat some other time," she said. "This food is for you alone."

The boy finished, then said, "Oh, grandmother, I am sleepy. I have to lie down now and get some rest," and with these words he wrapped himself in an old piece of skin and began to snore as if he were sound asleep.

But the skin had a tiny hole in it, and through the hole the boy was watching to see what his grandmother would do.

When the old woman was satisfied
that her grandson was sleeping, she
took out a bark case from under her bed
and carefully opened it. Inside were
a tiny kettle, a red-willow wand, and a
piece of food. Holding the food in
her hand, she scraped off a few crumbs
into the kettle and added water.

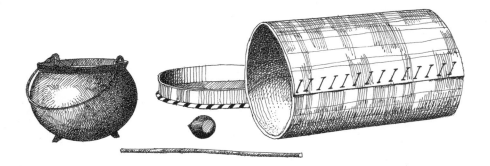

When it began to boil, she tapped
the kettle gently with the wand and
sang the words, "**Now, my kettle, I want
you to grow.**" As she sang, the kettle
became large and filled up with pudding.

She ate the pudding quickly, and as soon as she was finished, she washed the kettle, shook it to make it small again, then put everything back in the hiding place under her bed.

The next day, while the grandmother was out getting firewood, the boy searched under her bed until he found the things he had seen her use the night before. The tiny piece of food seemed hardly enough for one portion, so he scraped all of it into the kettle and began to tap with the wand.

The kettle became enormous. It grew so large the boy had to use a paddle to stir the pudding. As it boiled, making the sound **bub bub bub bub bub**, it began to overflow and fill the room around the fire.

Is the boy acting babyish or grown-up when he tries out his grandmother's magic?
(Circle your answer.)

BABYISH

GROWN-UP

The boy jumped onto the bed and kept stirring. Then he climbed to the rafters and finally to the roof. Running around the smoke hole, he kept on stirring the pudding, which now filled the entire lodge.

Suddenly he saw his grandmother hurrying out of the woods. Looking up, she could see her grandson running in circles on the roof. When she reached the door of the lodge, she saw the bark flaps bulging and the pudding already starting to spill out.

Immediately she blew on the pudding, and it shrank back. She blew harder. It shrank more, and she kept on blowing until it was all gone. Then she called to her grandson, "Come, now, get down from there."

Her voice was sad. As the boy
crawled off the roof, she said to him,
"You have used up all my food. There
is nothing else I can eat. That little
piece would have lasted me many years."

Wrapping herself in a skin robe,
she added, "I may as well lie down
right here. Hunger will finish me off."
Having said this, she lay on the ground
and covered herself up completely.

"Grandmother," cried the boy,
"what is the name of this food?"

"It is called chestnut," she said,
speaking through the robe.

"And where does it grow?"

"It is of no use for me to tell
you. How could you ever get to it? You
are only a little boy." Her voice was
muffled. But she continued, saying, "The
chestnut tree is owned by seven sisters,
who are witches, and the path to their
lodge is guarded by living things
that would attack you."

"And where is the path?"

"Toward the rising sun."

Then the boy left on a swift run. All day he raced, until the sun was low in the west and he saw as he passed through a clearing that the woods' edges were hidden in dew clouds. There he built a fire and camped for the night.

Standing close to the fire and holding a pinch of tobacco he had taken from his pouch, he said, "Come, now, listen to me, you, all kinds of animals and you, too, who have formed and made my life." With these words he threw the tobacco into the fire, then cried out, "Now, listen. The smoke is rising. I ask you to help me."

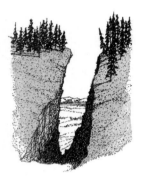

The next morning he started
early, hurrying on toward the east. It
wasn't long before he came to a steep
gorge, too steep to climb into and
too wide to jump across. Then he talked
to the gorge: "Earth, why are you
broken? This is unheard of. **I won't allow
it. Close up!**" And the earth closed
with a loud snap.

He kept on until he came to
two giant rattlesnakes standing guard
over the path. They opened their
jaws and began to rattle. But the boy
talked to them: "Rattlesnakes, go
away. **Get out of my path. Be ashamed!**"

Frightened, the rattlesnakes
closed their jaws and hurried off into
the woods.

The boy ran on. Suddenly two
panthers appeared, one on each
side of the path. He ran straight toward
them. "Panthers," he said, **"you are
free to go. Get out of my way!"**

Surprised by the boy's words,
the panthers drew back and let him pass.

He ran on, until at last the trees
began to thin out and he could see a
lodge in the distance at the far side of a
clearing. Next to the lodge stood the
chestnut tree, guarded by an eagle
perched at the top.

Why does the boy choose a mole to be his helper? (Underline one or two things on this page that help you answer this question.)

Knowing that he would have to be careful, the boy called for a mole, saying, "Now, my friend, I want you to come to me. Come to me, you mole." In a short time the leaves began to rustle at his feet, and a mole appeared, asking, "What do you want?"

The boy replied, "My grandmother is in trouble. I scraped away her last chestnut. Now you must help me get her some more. Let me fit inside your body. Take me underground to that tree in the far corner of the clearing, and don't let the eagle hear us."

When the boy had entered the mole's body, it made its way quickly to the roots of the tree. Then it pushed its nose and mouth up through the dry leaves, and the boy stuck his ear out of the mole's mouth to listen for sounds from the lodge.

The Boy in the Mole's Body

Hearing nothing, he jumped to his
full size, shook a bag from his pouch,
and filled it with chestnuts. He had turned
to go and was just running off when
the eagle heard him and gave a scream.

At once the seven sisters came
out of their lodge, waving their war clubs,
shouting, "Someone has stolen our
chestnuts. Catch him!"

The boy ran as fast as he could,
but the witches kept coming nearer. He
could hear their footsteps close behind
him. Suddenly he turned around and
began to beat on the bag of chestnuts
as though it were a drum. "Now you
will dance," he cried. And he sang:

> **to the upper side**
> **of the sky**
> **to the upper side**
> **of the sky**
> **and never return**
> **and never return**

He kept on drumming as the sisters rose into the air, half as high as the tallest trees, and all the while they were dancing. They rose still higher and soon disappeared in the sky.

The boy ran on, not stopping until the sun went under the hills and the black night came. Again he made camp, and in the morning he continued on his way, arriving at his grandmother's in time to hear her say, "Oh, grandson, you have come, and I am still alive." The boy rushed into the lodge, letting the bag of chestnuts fall—with the sound **pumh!** It was very heavy.

Why is the boy's magic stronger than the witches' magic?

"Grandson, tell me," cried the old woman, "how did you ever do it?"

"I, of course, know how I did it, but I will tell you only this: that I got rid of all those witches."

"So be it," she said. "What a wonderful thing this is." Then they scattered handfuls of chestnuts, and many were planted.

From that time on, the grandmother always had enough to eat, and somewhere, deep in the woods, they say, she is still making chestnut puddings.

The Chestnut-Scattering Chant

_____

_____

_____

_____

_____

_____

_____

_____

What a wonderful thing this is!

My Question _____

_____

_____

Name _____

THE PIED PIPER

ENGLISH FOLKTALE

The Rats of Franchville

Newtown, or Franchville, as 'twas
called of old, is a sleepy little town,
as you all may know, upon the Solent
shore. Sleepy as it is now, it was
once noisy enough, and what made the
noise was—rats. The place was so infested
with them as to be scarce worth living
in. There wasn't a barn or a cornrick,
a storeroom or a cupboard, but they
ate their way into it. Not a cheese but they
gnawed it hollow, not a sugar puncheon
but they cleared out. Why the very
mead and beer in the barrels was
not safe from them. They'd gnaw
a hole in the top of the tun, and down
would go one master rat's tail, and
when he brought it up round would
crowd all the friends and cousins,
and each would have a suck at the tail.

Had they stopped here it might
have been borne. But the squeaking and
shrieking, the hurrying and scurrying,
so that you could neither hear yourself
speak nor get a wink of good honest
sleep the livelong night! Not to mention
that, Mamma must needs sit up, and keep
watch and ward over baby's cradle,
or there'd have been a big ugly rat
running across the poor little fellow's face,
and doing who knows what mischief.

Why didn't the good people of the
town have cats? Well they did, and
there was a fair stand-up fight, but in the
end the rats were too many, and the
pussies were regularly driven from the
field. Poison, I hear you say? Why, they
poisoned so many that it fairly bred
a plague. Ratcatchers! Why there wasn't
a ratcatcher from John o' Groats'

House to the Land's End that hadn't
tried his luck. But do what they might,
cats or poison, terrier or traps, there
seemed to be more rats than ever,
and every day a fresh rat was cocking
his tail or pricking his whiskers.

The Mayor and the town council
were at their wits' end. As they were
sitting one day in the town hall racking
their poor brains, and bewailing
their hard fate, who should run in
but the town beadle. "Please your
Honour," says he, "here is a very

queer fellow come to town. I don't rightly
know what to make of him." "Show
him in," said the Mayor, and in he stepped.
A queer fellow, truly. For there wasn't
a colour of the rainbow but you might
find it in some corner of his dress,
and he was tall and thin, and had keen
piercing eyes.

"I'm called the Pied Piper," he began.
"And pray what might you be willing
to pay me, if I rid you of every single
rat in Franchville?"

Well, much as they feared the rats,
they feared parting with their money
more, and fain would they have higgled
and haggled. But the Piper was not a
man to stand nonsense, and the upshot
was that fifty pounds were promised him
(and it meant a lot of money in those
old days) as soon as not a rat was left to
squeak or scurry in Franchville.

Out of the hall stepped the Piper,
and as he stepped he laid his pipe to his
lips and a shrill keen tune sounded
through street and house. And as each
note pierced the air you might have seen
a strange sight. For out of every hole
the rats came tumbling. There were none
too old and none too young, none
too big and none too little to crowd at
the Piper's heels and with eager feet and
upturned noses to patter after him
as he paced the streets. Nor was the Piper
unmindful of the little toddling ones,
for every fifty yards he'd stop and give
an extra flourish on his pipe just to give
them time to keep up with the older
and stronger of the band.

Up Silver Street he went, and down Gold Street, and at the end of Gold Street is the harbour and the broad Solent beyond. And as he paced along, slowly and gravely, the townsfolk flocked to door and window, and many a blessing they called down upon his head.

As for getting near him there were too many rats. And now that he was at the water's edge he stepped into a boat, and not a rat, as he shoved off into deep water, piping shrilly all the while, but followed him, plashing, paddling, and wagging their tails with delight. On and on he played and played until the tide went down, and each master rat sank deeper and deeper in the slimy ooze of the harbour, until every mother's son of them was dead and smothered.

Do you feel sorry
for the rats?
(Circle your answer.)

YES   NO

Why or why not?

32

The tide rose again, and the
Piper stepped on shore, but never a rat
followed. You may fancy the townsfolk
had been throwing up their caps
and hurrahing and stopping up rat-holes
and setting the church bells a-ringing.
But when the Piper stepped ashore
and not so much as a single squeak
was to be heard, the Mayor and the
Council, and the townsfolk generally,
began to hum and to ha and to
shake their heads.

For the town money chest had been sadly emptied of late, and where was the fifty pounds to come from? Such an easy job, too! Just getting into a boat and playing a pipe! Why the Mayor himself could have done that if only he had thought of it.

So he hummed and ha'ad and at last, "Come, my good man," said he, "you see what poor folk we are; how can we manage to pay you fifty pounds? Will you not take twenty? When all is said and done 'twill be good pay for the trouble you've taken."

"Fifty pounds was what I bargained for," said the Piper shortly; "and if I were you I'd pay it quickly. For I can pipe many kinds of tunes, as folk sometimes find to their cost."

Do you think the Pied Piper should have accepted the twenty pounds? (Circle your answer.)

YES   NO

Why or why not?

34

"Would you threaten us, you
strolling vagabond?" shrieked the Mayor,
and at the same time he winked to
the Council; "the rats are all dead and
drowned," muttered he; and so "You may
do your worst, my good man," and
with that he turned short upon his heel.

"Very well," said the Piper, and
he smiled a quiet smile. With that he laid
his pipe to his lips afresh, but now
there came forth no shrill notes, as it
were, of scraping and gnawing, and
squeaking and scurrying, but the
tune was joyous and resonant, full of
happy laughter and merry play. And as he
paced down the streets the elders

mocked, but from schoolroom and
playroom, from nursery and workshop,
not a child but ran out with eager glee
and shout following gaily at the Piper's
call. Dancing, laughing, joining hands
and tripping feet, the bright throng moved
along up Gold Street and down Silver
Street, and beyond Silver Street lay
the cool green forest full of old oaks and
wide-spreading beeches. In and out
among the oak trees you might catch
glimpses of the Piper's many-coloured
coat. You might hear the laughter
of the children break and fade and die

away as deeper and deeper into the lone green wood the stranger went and the children followed.

All the while, the elders watched and waited. They mocked no longer now. And watch and wait as they might, never did they set their eyes again upon the Piper in his parti-coloured coat. Never were their hearts gladdened by the song and dance of the children issuing forth from amongst the ancient oaks of the forest.

Do you think
the townspeople
deserved to lose
their children?
(Circle your answer.)

YES   NO

Why or why not?

The children are imagining _____
_____

Greedy

Fair

Magical

Mean

Smart

Fun

Scary

The Pied Piper

Song of the Rats

We are the rats!

Listen to the sound of our _____

_____

_____

_____

_____

_____

My Question

Name

FANCIFUL ANIMALS

POETRY

THE
QUANGLE WANGLE'S
HAT

1

On the top of the Crumpetty Tree
    The Quangle Wangle sat,
But his face you could not see,
    On account of his Beaver Hat.
For his Hat was a hundred and two feet wide,
With ribbons and bibbons on every side
And bells, and buttons, and loops, and lace,
So that nobody ever could see the face
    Of the **Quangle Wangle Quee.**

2

The Quangle Wangle said
    To himself on the Crumpetty Tree,
"Jam; and jelly; and bread;
    Are the best food for me!
But the longer I live on this Crumpetty Tree
The plainer than ever it seems to me
That very few people come this way
And that life on the whole is far from gay!"
    Said the **Quangle Wangle Quee**.

3

But there came to the Crumpetty Tree,
    Mr. and Mrs. Canary;
And they said, "Did you ever see
    Any spot so charmingly airy?
May we build a nest on your lovely Hat?
Mr. Quangle Wangle, grant us that!
O please let us come and build a nest
Of whatever material suits you best,
    Mr. **Quangle Wangle Quee!**"

Why doesn't the
Quangle Wangle
take off his hat?
(Circle one.)
1. He's shy
2. Quangle Wangles
always wear big
hats
3. He's proud of
his hat
4. He's afraid
5. The hat is part
of his head
6. Other _____
_____
_____

45

4

And besides, to the Crumpetty Tree
    Came the Stork, the Duck, and the Owl;
The Snail, and the Bumble-Bee,
    The Frog, and the Fimble Fowl;
(The Fimble Fowl, with a Corkscrew leg;)
And all of them said, "We humbly beg,
    We may build our homes on your lovely Hat,
Mr. Quangle Wangle, grant us that!
    Mr. **Quangle Wangle Quee!**"

Pretend you are
the Quangle Wangle
telling the other
animals they can
live on your hat.
What do you think
the Quangle Wangle
said?

5

And the Golden Grouse came there,
   And the Pobble who has no toes,
And the small Olympian bear,
   And the Dong with a luminous nose.
And the Blue Baboon, who played the flute,
And the Orient Calf from the Land of Tute,
And the Attery Squash, and the Bisky Bat,
All came and built on the lovely Hat
   Of the **Quangle Wangle Quee**.

6

And the Quangle Wangle said
   To himself on the Crumpetty Tree,
"When all these creatures move
   What a wonderful noise there'll be!"
And at night by the light of the Mulberry moon
They danced to the Flute of the Blue Baboon,
On the broad green leaves of the Crumpetty Tree,
And all were as happy as happy could be,
   With the **Quangle Wangle Quee**.

—**Edward Lear**

Why does the
Quangle Wangle
enjoy having a noisy
party on his hat?

My Made-Up Animal

My Question

_____

_____

_____

Name _____

THE OWL
AND THE PUSSY-CAT

1

The Owl and the Pussy-cat went to sea
In a beautiful pea-green boat,
They took some honey, and plenty of money,
Wrapped up in a five-pound note.
The Owl looked up to the stars above,
And sang to a small guitar,
"O lovely Pussy! O Pussy, my love,
What a beautiful Pussy you are,
You are,
You are!
What a beautiful Pussy you are!"

2

Pussy said to the Owl, "You elegant fowl!

   How charmingly sweet you sing!

O let us be married! too long we have tarried:

   But what shall we do for a ring?"

They sailed away, for a year and a day,

   To the land where the Bong-tree grows

And there in a wood a Piggy-wig stood

   With a ring at the end of his nose,

      His nose,

      His nose,

With a ring at the end of his nose.

3

"Dear Pig, are you willing to sell for one shilling
    Your ring?" Said the Piggy, "I will."
So they took it away, and were married next day
    By the Turkey who lives on the hill.
They dined on mince, and slices of quince,
    Which they ate with a runcible spoon;
And hand in hand, on the edge of the sand,
    They danced by the light of the moon,
        The moon,
        The moon,
They danced by the light of the moon.

—Edward Lear

TEDDY BEAR

1

A bear, however hard he tries,
Grows tubby without exercise.
Our Teddy Bear is short and fat
Which is not to be wondered at;
He gets what exercise he can
By falling off the ottoman,
But generally seems to lack
The energy to clamber back.

2

Now tubbiness is just the thing
Which gets a fellow wondering;
And Teddy worried lots about
The fact that he was rather stout.
He thought: "If only I were thin!
But how does anyone begin?"
He thought: "It really isn't fair
To grudge me exercise and air."

3

For many weeks he pressed in vain
His nose against the window-pane,
And envied those who walked about
Reducing their unwanted stout.
None of the people he could see
"Is quite" (he said) "as fat as me!"
Then, with a still more moving sigh,
"I mean" (he said) "as fat as I!"

4

Now Teddy, as was only right,
Slept in the ottoman at night,
And with him crowded in as well
More animals than I can tell;
Not only these, but books and things,
Such as a kind relation brings—
Old tales of "Once upon a time,"
And history retold in rhyme.

5

One night it happened that he took
A peep at an old picture-book,
Wherein he came across by chance
The picture of a King of France
(A stoutish man) and, down below,
These words: "King Louis So and So,
Nicknamed 'The Handsome!'" There he sat,
And (think of it!) the man was __fat__!

6

Our bear rejoiced like anything
To read about this famous King,
Nicknamed "The Handsome." There he sat
And certainly the man was **fat**.
Nicknamed "The Handsome." Not a doubt
The man was definitely **stout**.
Why then, a bear (for all his tub)
Might yet be named "**The Handsome Cub!**"

7

"Might yet be named." Or did he mean
That years ago he "might have been"?
For now he felt a slight misgiving:
"Is Louis So and So still living?
Fashions in beauty have a way
Of altering from day to day.
Is 'Handsome Louis' with us yet?
Unfortunately I forget."

8

Next morning (nose to window-pane)
The doubt occurred to him again.
One question hammered in his head:
"Is he alive or is he dead?"
Thus, nose to pane, he pondered; but
The lattice window, loosely shut,
Swung open. With one startled "Oh!"
Our Teddy disappeared below.

9

There happened to be passing by
A plump man with a twinkling eye,
Who, seeing Teddy in the street,
Raised him politely to his feet,
And murmured kindly in his ear
Soft words of comfort and of cheer:
"Well, well!" "Allow me!" "Not at all."
"Tut-tut! A very nasty fall."

10

Our Teddy answered not a word;
It's doubtful if he even heard.
Our bear could only look and look:
The stout man in the picture-book!
That "handsome" King—could this be he,
This man of adiposity?
"Impossible," he thought. "But still,
No harm in asking. Yes I will!"

11

"Are you," he said, "by any chance
His Majesty the King of France?"
The other answered, "I am that,"
Bowed stiffly, and removed his hat;
Then said, "Excuse me," with an air,
"But is it Mr. Edward Bear?"
And Teddy, bending very low,
Replied politely, "Even so!"

12

They stood beneath the window there,

The King and Mr. Edward Bear,

And, handsome, if a trifle fat,

Talked carelessly of this and that...

Then said His Majesty, "Well, well,

I must get on," and rang the bell.

"Your bear, I think," he smiled. "Good-day!"

And turned, and went upon his way.

13

A bear, however hard he tries,

Grows tubby without exercise.

Our Teddy Bear is short and fat,

Which is not to be wondered at.

But do you think it worries him

To know that he is far from slim?

No, just the other way about—

He's *proud* of being short and stout.

—A. A. Milne

My Favorite Words

Acknowledgments

—

All possible care has been taken to trace ownership and secure permission for each selection in this series. The Great Books Foundation wishes to thank the following authors, publishers, and representatives for permission to reprint the copyrighted material in this volume:

Chestnut Pudding, from THE NAKED BEAR: FOLKTALES OF THE IROQUOIS, by John Bierhorst. Copyright 1987 by John Bierhorst. Reprinted by permission of William Morrow & Co.

"Teddy Bear," from WHEN WE WERE VERY YOUNG, by A. A. Milne. Copyright 1924 by E. P. Dutton; renewed 1952 by A. A. Milne. Reprinted by permission of Dutton Children's Books, a division of Penguin Books USA, Inc.

Illustration Credits

—

David Cunningham prepared the illustrations for *Chestnut Pudding.*

Michael Carroll prepared the illustrations for *The Pied Piper.*

Diane Cole prepared the illustration for *"The Quangle Wangle's Hat."*

Edward Lear's illustrations for *"The Owl and the Pussy-Cat"* were reproduced courtesy of the Newberry Library.

Ernest Shepard's illustrations for *"Teddy Bear"* are from WHEN WE WERE VERY YOUNG. Reprinted by permission of Dutton Children's Books, a division of Penguin Books USA, Inc. Reproduced courtesy of the Newberry Library. Illustration on page 60 by William Seabright.

"G.B." was created by Ed Young. Copyright 1990 by Ed Young.

Cover art by David Frampton.

Cover and book design by William Seabright and Paul Uhl, Design Associates.